Walking
G~~with~~randfather

Walking with Grandfather

THE WISDOM OF LAKOTA ELDERS

Joseph M. Marshall III

SOUNDS TRUE

Sounds True, Inc., Boulder, CO 80306
© 2005 Joseph M. Marshall III

SOUNDS TRUE is a trademark of Sounds True, Inc.

The illustrations for this book are by Roberta Collier-Morales
and are reproduced by permission.

Cover photo © Bob Rowan; Progressive Image/CORBIS.

Jacket and book design by Rachael Tomich.

Published 2005
Printed in Korea

ISBN 1-59179-352-1
Library of Congress Control Number: 2005931983

Also by Joseph M. Marshall III from Sounds True:
Quiet Thunder: The Wisdom of Crazy Horse 6-CD audio learning program

*Dedicated to grandparents
and elders everywhere*

Table of Contents

INTRODUCTION   The Greatest of the Greatest:
A Treatise on Wisdom   1

1   The Trail to Yesterday: The Importance of Identity   15

2   The Way of Wolves   27

3   The Greyhound   41

4   The Bow and the Arrow   53

5   The Shadow Man   65

6   Follow Me   77

7   The Circle of Life   87

8   The End of the Journey Is the Beginning   99

AFTERWORD   The Wisdom Within   107

ABOUT THE AUTHOR   115

The Greatest of the Greatest: A Treatise on Wisdom

Toss a pebble into a pond and the waves flow outward in ever-growing circles. That is a physical reality.

In the Lakota encampments of old, the biggest and tallest lodge stood in the very center of the encampment. There the elders met.

The oldest men in the village formed the council of elders. There was one basic requirement: Obviously, one had to be old.

Try to imagine the number of years of experience represented by the village council. Depending on the size of the village, this could vary from hundreds to thousands of years. Yet, the council had no authority. As a matter of fact, there really is no word for *authority* in the Lakota language. So, how did the council of elders fulfill its responsibility?

The council of elders fulfilled its responsibility through the power of the influence of their wisdom.

Various matters of concern and importance were brought to the council—from everyday life issues to matters of war. Every issue was discussed at length, sometimes for several days and nights. At the end, the council didn't issue ultimatums or edicts. They simply informed the people what they thought. That opinion, or opinions, was the basis for action because of the depth of the council's wisdom.

The Lakota consider fortitude, generosity, bravery, and wisdom to be the four greatest virtues. In any discussion or mention of these virtues, wisdom is invariably the last to be named. However intentional or unintentional that may be, it is entirely appropriate because wisdom is not only the greatest of the four greatest, it is also the most difficult to achieve. Furthermore, wisdom is associated with old age, and that, too, is entirely appropriate because wisdom cannot be had in ten easy lessons. One has to live a long life to gain wisdom, and it is regarded as life's gift by some who finally achieve it. It is, many also realize, a gift they cannot keep to themselves. It must be given back to life.

What, then, *is* wisdom?

Just as knowledge is derived from information, wisdom begins with knowledge, grows with experience, and is empowered by discernment.

On the other hand, wisdom is one of those realities of life that is best perceived by the effect it has, like the wind. Wind cannot be seen, but its movement is visible when an entire hillside of grass bends in the same direction. It cannot be touched, but anyone who feels it stir on a hot day can feel the relief it brings. Wind does not speak, but it can give whispery voice to the branches of a red cedar tree. Therefore, we know wind exists. Hence, we know wisdom exists. We know it is an ancient virtue, but at times it seems difficult to see its effect on our society and our world. Sometimes its absence seems more evident.

Someone said, "The greatest arrogance of the present is to forget the intelligence of the past." The author of that statement obviously understood that we contemporary humans, especially in American society, think that all that matters is the present. We forget, or just plain don't know, how we got where we are today, intellectually, morally, philosophically, and technologically. We live in a world that moves at cyber speed, craves instant gratification, and revels in technology. Consequently, we are so impressed with the current version of ourselves that we aren't aware that our ancestors contributed to what we are and what we do and how we think. For example, as we ride in our sedans and SUVs, some of us may have some inkling that automobiles were invented within the past 120 years. But fewer of us probably know that the wheel was invented hundreds of years before that. Fewer still would realize that the wheel enabled the invention of carts, wagons, buggies, and other wheeled conveyances that are the forerunners of our automobiles.

Astonishingly, there is a mind-set that technology of the past was crude and imprecise. Those who think so would be startled to discover that modern-day surveyors have learned that mind-set to be a fallacy. A few years ago, survey coordinates done in the days of George Washington were checked by surveyors using satellite-aided global positioning instruments. They were surprised to learn that the surveyors of the mid-1700s were off in their measurements—when they were off at all—by no more than six inches.

If we sometimes disdain the mechanical or technological abilities of our ancestors, we also have a tendency to turn up our noses at their beliefs and philosophies, describing them as "quaint" or "archaic." The spiritual views of some northern Plains tribes in regard to *death serving life* are a case in point.

Many primitive cultures all over the world believe that death separates the spirit (or the soul) from the body and that the spirit and the body each serve a different purpose thereafter. Among many indigenous societies in North America, a special ceremony was usually conducted to release the spirit of a person who died so it could go on to the next life. In the meantime, burial practices enabled the body to return to the Earth, practically speaking.

Among the tribes of the northern Plains, the deceased was enclosed in a hide and placed atop a wooden scaffold (a platform supported by poles) or sometimes in a large tree. After several years, when it was obvious that the body had shrunk inside the hide encasement from decomposition, it was taken down and buried in the ground. Thereafter, the process of decomposition was completed, and the remains became part of the Earth. We now know, biologically, that organic material is reduced to basic components—such as carbon—as decomposition occurs, and these compounds become nutrients on which new plant life feeds. The "quaint" and "archaic" belief of death serving life is a reality.

Modern technology and the astounding tasks that gadgets can perform have effectively blinded us to the intelligence of our ancestors. We've become arrogant as a society and as a nation. And if we look with disdain on one aspect of the past, we have a strong tendency to assume that our ancestors were somehow lacking across the board. We then characterize everything about the past as "quaint" and "archaic," and we forget the value and power of wisdom. Of all the mistakes we could make, that is arguably the worst.

And if anything in our society should be synonymous with wisdom, it should unequivocally be leadership.

Here, once again, the intelligence of the past offers some insights and perhaps some lessons as well, depending on how arrogant and self-absorbed we are.

Up to the reservation era, wisdom was an inherent part of the leadership in Lakota society. Wisdom was more important than authority. As a matter of fact, there was no authority. As another matter of fact, there was no concept of authority.

Euro-American thinking forces non-Indians to assume that without "law and order," societies cannot be governed. Contrary to such assumptions, indigenous societies of North America did "govern" themselves, although there were no written laws or codes or rules as such. Indigenous societies did have expectations and rules for behavior, but just as important, they looked to the wisdom of the elders among them.

Many tribes had a process that had worked for many generations, and some were more structured than others. The Cheyenne, for example, had (and still have) the Council of Forty-Four. For most tribes, however, the hierarchy of government was informal, and at the core—in terms of influence—was usually a council of elderly men. In Lakota, they were called, as a group, *wica omniciyapi*, or the "council of (complete) men"—with *complete men* meaning men who had experienced and accomplished much in their lives and who were unselfish, humble, and wise. Another term for them was *woglaka wicasa*, meaning "the men who speak (for the people)." This label was not given as a sort of job description for the men of the council to follow. Rather, it described them, because their first concern was for the welfare of the people and they would address or speak to that issue first and foremost.

The council of elders did not pass legislation or issue edicts. Their primary purpose was to discuss each and every issue, concern, and problem at length. After discussion, the council would usually arrive at an opinion regarding the issue or question at hand. That opinion was revealed to the people, who accepted it as advice and counsel, rather than as a directive or an order. But the people understood that the council's opinion had the weight of several hundred years of life experiences and the wisdom the council possessed individually and collectively. Therefore, much more often than not, the advice of the council was followed.

While the *wica omniciyapi* was the overall deliberative body for each community, there were also other leaders who could generally be categorized as civilian or military. In either case, individuals selected as leaders were chosen on the basis of their common sense, a sound record of achievement and good judgment, and compassion. Now and then, men who excelled as battlefield leaders were also called upon to lead in civilian life. To be sure, there were men who aspired to be leaders primarily because of the prestige, but many served because they sincerely cared about the welfare of the people. To keep a position of leadership, a man had to put the needs of the people before his own and make good decisions. There were no terms of office. If a man did his job well, the people continued to follow him. If he was a poor leader, the people simply stopped following. It was not unusual for such a poor leader to wake up one morning and find that the people had moved away from him during the night. The will of the people, as it were. The ousted leader couldn't cry foul because of a technicality or a glitch in the voting process. And there was no supreme court in the land that could overturn or interfere with that vote.

One leader who enjoyed the loyalty and confidence of the people until the moment of his death was Sitting Bull, the Hunkpapa Lakota. At the height of his influence as a leader, he called for a gathering of all the Lakota groups. At the time, the total population was around 20,000. They began gathering in May of that year, and by the end of June, 8,000 people had come together to discuss issues of national concern—mainly, the encroachment of Euro-Americans into Lakota territory and its undesirable consequences. During that gathering, Lakota fighting men fought to a standstill or outright defeated two separate units of the U.S. Army. The year was 1876, and the last of the two battles was fought at the Little Bighorn River against the U.S. Seventh Cavalry.

The worth of a leader is measured, or should be measured, by the depth of true loyalty and respect exhibited for him (or her) by the people. How many other leaders, past or present, on this continent can state unequivocally that nearly half of the nation answered their call? Perhaps a better question is, Why? Why did 8,000 out of 20,000 respond to Sitting Bull's call to gather in the summer of 1876?

By 1876, Sitting Bull was at the pinnacle of his influence as a leader. He had, or demonstrated, all the requisite qualities. His record of achievements as a warrior was considerable. As a medicine man, he exemplified selflessness and compassion, but he was also an astute politician and a skilled orator. It would have been easy for him to assume the mantle of arrogance and make himself more important than his family, his community, and his nation. But he knew that the true worth of a man was measured by what he did for the people.

Sitting Bull's actions were motivated foremost by his concern for the good of the nation, hence the people, and not by a need to keep his job or to keep an eye on his popularity ratings. The people knew that Sitting Bull was a wise man, not so much because he could draw on his own wisdom, but because he didn't hesitate to seek it from *his elders*.

Sitting Bull could join the other elders in the center of the village. Where, today, are our elders? Have we placed them in the center of the village so that their experience and insight, their wisdom, can flow outward? Look around and see for yourself where our elders are.

What happens to those of us who do not seek or heed the wisdom of the elders?

LONG AGO—a very long time ago—a group of Lakota were traveling across the prairie. They were walking because it was the time before horses. Household goods were carried by dogs pulling drag poles and in backpacks carried by strong young men and women. On the flanks of the column were the warriors as the first line of defense. Leading the column was the old man leader and an old medicine man.

A shout came from one of the warriors in the rear. Everyone turned to see smoke and flames coming from behind. A prairie fire, one of the most frightening and devastating forces on the northern Plains, was coming. The people panicked; the flames were tall and moving swiftly. Instinctively, everyone ran.

Soon it was obvious that the flames were coming much too fast. The people looked for water, a creek or a small lake they could jump into, but there was nothing close by. Backpacks were tossed aside, and dogs were freed from their burdens so they could run freely. The stronger men and women grabbed the smaller children and the feebler old people. There was nothing to do but run as fast as possible.

But after an exhausting run, the heat of the ever-growing flames became intense. Everyone knew they couldn't outrun the flames. Children cried, and everyone shouted. Then, a quiet voice was heard amid the din and confusion.

"We must run back through the flames!"

An old woman had spoken.

The people were aghast. Immediately, however, many saw the wisdom in her words. But some didn't because they were too afraid.

Older elders gathered around and quickly advised everyone to pour what water was in flasks over the clothing of the children. So it was done as the flames rushed closer and closer and the smoke blocked out the sun. The thought of running back through the flames was utterly terrifying, but it was the only hope. But some didn't see it that way and kept running away.

The old woman who had spoken first was also the first to run back through the flames. Mothers and fathers gathered their children to them, and many followed her into the jaws of death itself.

Several people died, mostly the very old or the very young whose lungs couldn't stand the intense heat. One of them was the old woman who had led the way. But of those who braved the flames, many did survive. They were all scarred, however, on their legs and thighs. So thereafter they called themselves the *Sicangu Oyate*, the Burnt Thigh People. Today, we are the Sicangu Lakota, one of the seven bands of the Lakota. We are more commonly known as the Rosebud Sioux.

We will never forget the courage of our ancestors and how they earned the name we will always have. And we will never forget that it was the wisdom of an old woman that saved her people.

Needless to say, the people who didn't heed her wisdom all died a horrible death.

SO, LET US ASK AGAIN, where are our elders today?

Sadly, if we are honest, we know where they are not.

They are not in the center of the village. Their wisdom is not flowing outward.

Any person or society or nation that ignores the lessons of the past will—sooner or later—face the flames of their own fears or arrogance. Some may not survive.

Isn't it time, then, to put the elders back in the center of the village?

1

The Trail to Yesterday: The Importance of Identity

Taking walks with my grandfather shaped my life.

In real time, those walks happened more than fifty years ago, but in my memory, they occur any time I want to relive them.

Taking walks with my grandfather was much more than getting from one place to another. The intimacy we formed with the land is unforgettable, of course. But now, as I am approaching that place he was in his life during those walks, I realize that I was walking with wisdom.

His name was Albert, a Sicangu Lakota. He was in his sixties when I came into his life. His shoulders were wide, his arms strong, and his energy nearly boundless. I watched him build a log house, virtually without help. When I was big enough, I helped him harness the horses that pulled our wagon. He taught me how to hunt and how to make bows and arrows. Grandpa Albert could do anything, and I wanted to be like him. Now I have grandchildren of my own, and I'm beginning to realize a fact imperceptible to me as a younger person. It wasn't so much what Grandpa Albert could do that made him unique. Rather his essence as a human being was how he had lived and the insights into life that he had earned because of what he had learned and experienced. He had earned life's gift: wisdom.

Needless to say, I learned much from my grandfather, and not only during my childhood. I can and do recall the valuable lessons he taught, of course, because they are in my file of memories. Interestingly, however, there are moments when something that he said or did will suddenly reveal itself, something that—up until a given moment—I had apparently forgotten. But those memories reappear, as it were, because a current moment gives them meaning. Or, more to the point, a certain statement or piece of advice or an action from the past gives meaning and clarity to the current moment.

For example, not long ago, I watched several television commercials as they came fast and furious in the weeks just before the election. To me, there was no difference among them. One commercial tore down one candidate's record of service and reputation, while another tried to build it up. The commercials reminded me of something that my grandfather had said more than once.

A truly humble person rarely stumbles, he contended, because such a person walks with his face toward the Earth and therefore can see the path ahead. An arrogant person walks with head held high to bask in the glory of the moment. Such a person is likely to stumble because he or she is more concerned with the moment than with what lies ahead. Grandpa Albert's advice was to align oneself with the humble person. If there was a truly humble person in the milieu of vociferous and contentious candidates, that person was lost in the process.

But the first and most enduring lesson from both my grandparents was about identity. Who and what we are as individuals, as a community, as a society, and as a nation, are the strengths and weaknesses with which we face and live life. And what we contribute to the identity of the whole begins with each of us individually. Grandpa Albert illustrated that to me early on.

A child first experiences the tangible. On the walks I took with my grandfather, my first impressions and more obvious memories are first and foremost of the physical environment, the variety of grasses, trees, birds, animals, and so on. Yet the less tangible memories often leave the more indelible impressions.

A river now called the Little White meandered lazily in the valley below my grandmother's land. The log house my grandfather built stood on a plateau north of it. Grandpa Albert called the river *Makizita Wakpa*, the Smoking Earth River. The Lakota named it so because of the smoky mists that hung over the river just after dawn during early spring and late autumn. Many of our walks, in all seasons of the year, were in the valley on either side of this river.

Some of our walks had another purpose. We would look for our horses, or we would pile dried wood, for cooking and heating, which we would later haul with the wagon. Sometimes we would fish in the quiet eddies of the river. Whatever the reason or purpose, Grandpa Albert would make sure that I was paying close attention to the journey itself, no matter how long or short it was. I still vividly recall the first time he pointed out a perfect circle of matted grass, about two feet in diameter, among some chokecherry shrubs.

I couldn't imagine what could cause such an imprint. Was it the single footprint of one of the giants in my grandmother's stories? To my initial disappointment, it was nothing so scary or dramatic. The circle of matted grass had been made by a white-tailed deer, probably the day before we had come along. During the day, the deer had slept there, hidden among the chokecherry shrubs, curled up in a ball. At night, it had left its bed to browse, since deer are nocturnal grazers.

This was my first lesson as a hunter. If you hunt the deer, you must know the deer. All along the trails, there were lessons such as that.

But the one lesson that has helped me through several difficult moments in my life is about the trail itself.

Grandpa Albert had a habit of stopping now and then and looking back down the trail. Frequently, he would take me by the shoulders and ask me to look back at the way we had come. "Remember the trail," he said, "because one of these times I will send you back alone. If you don't remember the way you have come, you will be lost."

That was my first lesson about identity.

Who and what we are is a work in progress. Life shapes us constantly, day in and day out. Life is obviously the trail we walk. No one is exempt; therefore, no one is unaffected by what happens along the way. But we don't start off on the trail with nothing.

None of us choose to be born, Grandpa Albert would remind me. Therefore, when and where we come into the world is quite by accident. But we do come into the world as something tangible. Each of us have a mother and a father. Each of our parents give us our physical identity and a host of inherent ethnic and cultural traits. That is the *who* that we are. And thereafter the family we are born into and/or that nurtures us gives us the foundation for *what* we will be.

My grandparents, Albert and Annie, were never uncertain as to who and what they were. In spite of being born into the middle of difficult—to say the least—societal changes, their sense of identity never wavered. Their parents understood that the best way to face the changes forced on the Lakota people, who had to give up the free-roaming, nomadic, hunting lifestyle for the limited existence on a reservation, was to hang on tenaciously to who and what they were. It was a lesson not totally lost on my grandparents' generation. It was the lesson my maternal grandparents passed on to me. They never let me forget where I had come from, so when it was my turn to face the trail on my own, I didn't lose my way.

The question often asked of Lakota and other native people, then and now, was: How do you live in two worlds? There is an implication in the question, an assumption that native people—because of the consequence of native and European interaction—had lost their sense of identity. Some did, of course, but others like my grandparents, did not.

There are, therefore, two answers to the question. If we Lakota (and other native people) did have our identities confused by the process of assimilation into another culture, we often didn't know which world we belonged in. Although many of us did learn to speak English and make other seemingly necessary changes, we knew we would never be exactly like white people—a fact that white people consistently pointed out to us. On the other hand, if we gave up our cultural identity, we could never fit back into our own ethnicity and culture. Therefore, we were never quite white and not really native (Indian) any longer.

My grandparents taught me that there was a better way to face this dilemma. They taught me to survive and function in a white-dominated society *as a Lakota*. In other words, learning to speak English and adapting the habits of the white people didn't mean I had to forsake *being* Lakota. All I had to do was adapt. Adapting is not the same as wholesale change.

My grandparents also taught me that people and circumstances would continuously try to change my sense of identity. And the best and only way to face that was to remember who I am. They illustrated their point with one of the first stories of *Iktomi*, or the Trickster, that I can recall hearing.

LONG AGO, IKTOMI CRAWLED OUT OF HIS DEN in a hillside on a fine beautiful day and decided to take a walk. At the bottom of a hill, he came to a pond with sparkling blue water. He lay down on his stomach at the edge to take a drink. Suddenly, a face appeared below him, a familiar face, mimicking everything he did. If Iktomi raised his eyebrows, the face in the pond did the same. After several moments, he realized the face was his.

Iktomi spent the rest of the day admiring his reflection. After the sun went down, he returned to his den. The next morning, the wind was blowing as Iktomi arrived at the pond, and he was dismayed to find that his reflection in the water was distorted. As the day wore on, the wind blew harder, and Iktomi's image in the water didn't improve. Angry and confused, he stomped home.

Bright and early the next morning, he awoke to a cold, rainy day. Nevertheless, he hurried to the pond. The reflection he saw in the water was nothing more than a shadow. Confused, he trudged back to his den.

The following day, the rain had stopped, but dark clouds filled the sky. Iktomi saw his reflection in the pond, but it was of a dark and angry face. He was about to slink away in anger when he heard laughter. Fox was giggling at Iktomi's confusion. Then Fox explained, or tried to explain, that the images were different because of the wind, the rain, and the dark clouds. But Iktomi didn't listen, choosing instead to hang on to his anger and confusion. He never could figure out which of the reflections in the pond was really him.

IF WE DON'T KNOW who and what we are, we'll likely react exactly like Iktomi when the reflection of ourselves gives us changes now and then. Unless we are aware that there is a basic core to who and what we are, we will see only the image that others see as us. That will cause us to be angry, frightened, and confused.

Some of the trails that my Grandpa Albert and I walked are still there. They are old trails, even ancient, perhaps laid out by the bison or the deer in some bygone age. Many of the trails are changed or grown over and not easy to see any longer, but they are easy to remember.

Such is life. The tracks we leave on the land will disappear over time. The tracks we leave in the hearts and minds of others will never fade.

I can still see my Grandpa Albert walking ahead of me. He was very vigorous for a man in his sixties. And I can recall having to trot and even run to keep up now and then. In much the same way, some of the things he tried to teach me were difficult for a boy of six or seven to understand. But I am beginning to understand more and more now. Overall, it's an awesome feeling.

There were moments when Grandpa would stop just at the crest of a hill. Then he would turn to me and ask: "Are you ready to see beyond the hill?"

I'm on the verge of being an elder, and I can't wait to see what is over that hill, because it's where my Grandpa was taking me all along.

It's part of who and what I am and am still becoming. I'm still a work in progress.

2

The Way of Wolves

As a child, there were no wolves in my world, but they were there in the stories my grandparents and others told. So I waited for one to cross my path someday. But not a single wolf did I ever see, anywhere.

One day, as we were walking along the Smoking Earth River, I suddenly asked my grandfather about wolves. More to the point, I asked him where the wolves lived.

"Only in the stories," was his reply. Then we sat down to rest in the shade of an oak tree, and he told me that the last wolf on the reservation had been killed in 1917, long before I was born.

He seemed to sense my sadness at hearing that bit of news, but I was also confused. Why would anyone want to kill wolves? He sensed the question as well and explained that most people who were not Lakota, or any other kind of native, were terrified of wolves. In their world and in their thinking, wolves were evil. That, apparently, drove them to kill any and all wolves.

As anger and confusion swirled in my mind, my grandfather quietly launched into a story about a woman who once lived with wolves.

LONG AGO, BEFORE THE COMING OF HORSES, a man brought home a second wife. His first wife was not only surprised; she was also hurt and angry because she thought she was being replaced. A man having more than one wife was not unusual in those days, though not every man took a second wife. Still, most men who did made certain the first wife was in agreement. But that didn't happen in this case.

The first wife couldn't get over her anger. Although it was late autumn, she made plans to leave her husband and live with relatives in another village. Even in the days before horses, the Lakota moved their villages often, so though the woman knew the general area where her relatives lived, she didn't know exactly where they were. Nonetheless, emboldened by her anger, she packed warm robes and food, filled water flasks, and set out.

Her husband's village was near the Black Hills, and her relatives lived to the east, near the Great Muddy River. The woman would have to travel many, many days across the prairie country, across lands inhabited by all manner of four-legged creatures, not to mention any two-legged enemies that might be about. She feared snakes and bears the most, however. Like all Lakota, men or women, she knew the land, but she had never traveled alone. At night, she made sheltered camps with small, hidden fires. During the day, she was especially careful when crossing over ridges and hills, just in case an enemy was watching.

After many days, she had not seen any fresh trails to indicate that she was close to her relatives' village, or any village for that matter. Her food supply was diminishing. Although she could set snares for rabbits and squirrels, it was the cold autumn winds that worried her the most. They were telling her that winter was coming soon. Her fears came to pass when snow began to fall one morning. By late afternoon, the snow covered the ground, bringing with it a biting cold. The woman was forced to find shelter in a hillside den.

It was always difficult to predict how long the first snow would fall. The woman had to wait in the den for several days because the snowfall didn't stop. When it did, the snow was deep. Though she scrounged firewood and dried buffalo chips to keep a small fire going, she had eaten all her food. As her hunger grew, so did her despair. She realized that she was foolish to travel alone, especially with winter on the way. But there was nothing to do but wait in the den.

She burned all the twigs and buffalo chips. Without a fire, the cold crept into the den. All she could do was huddle beneath her robes. After a time, however, she couldn't stop shivering.

One night, she fell into a fitful sleep and dreamed that a wolf had crawled into the den with her. When she awoke, she was startled to find not one wolf but several. They were curled up around her, and she realized they were keeping her warm.

The woman was not afraid of wolves, because she had never heard of any wolf doing harm to a two-legged. But she couldn't help but wonder why they weren't afraid of her.

She was even more surprised when yet another wolf arrived with a freshly killed rabbit in her jaws and left it for her. When the woman proceeded to build a fire, after she had skinned and butchered the rabbit, the wolves retreated from the den. But a few stayed nearby. The next morning, those that had left returned with a deer and left it at the mouth of the den.

Though she wondered why the wolves were being kind to her, the woman did not refuse their gifts of food. They, in turn, stayed nearby. At night, a few slept in the den with her while others went out, and she knew they were hunting.

Days went by. Winter came early and kept the land in a cold, icy grip. The woman knew that staying in and near the den was the wise thing to do. In the evenings and often during the night, she could hear wolves in the distance as they hunted. She began to recognize the different voices, and later, she began to understand the different messages they were conveying. She could tell if the hunting had gone well or not. She could distinguish when they were playful and when they were serious. Most of all, she realized that the wolves who had befriended her were all part of the same family. And though she was lonely and missed her husband and her relatives, she enjoyed the company of the wolf family and began to love them as she did her own.

She stayed with them through the winter, and as the months went by, she learned to bark and howl and sing as they did, and she often joined in. Winter passed, as she knew it would, and soon the wolves told her that a village of two-leggeds was moving and would pass close to them. They would take her so she could rejoin her kind, they said. So the woman prepared to find her relatives.

The woman and the entire family of wolves traveled to a high hill on a fine spring morning. There in a shallow valley below was a village. Sadly, the woman left her wolf family and walked down into the valley. There she found her relatives who were overjoyed to see her, because they had gotten word that the woman was lost and likely dead.

Over time, the woman and her husband were reunited. He had given up his second wife. By and by, the woman told her story of being saved by wolves, and no one was inclined to disbelieve her. As a matter of fact, she became known as Woman Who Lived With Wolves.

During many evenings, in all seasons of the year, Woman Who Lived With Wolves would listen as wolves spoke in the distance. She would smile as she recognized the voices of her wolf family. The wolves, in turn, would give her news, and they once warned her of enemies coming.

Woman Who Lived With Wolves had a long life, with children and grandchildren. She was known as a loving mother and a grandmother to all the children in the village. When she died, a family of wolves came to her burial scaffold and kept vigil through the night, occasionally singing a mourning song. They were gone with the morning sun, but on many nights, they could still be heard singing for the woman who had lived as one of them.

MY GRANDFATHER WAS RIGHT. Wolves still live. Fortunately, they have not all been wiped off the face of the Earth. But in some parts of this nation, they do live only in stories. There are still no wolves in the wild on the Rosebud Sioux Reservation, and they have been gone for so long that many native people have begun to forget what wolves were all about. Some even believe the Euro-American horror stories about wolves, about them being the epitome of evil. As my grandfather demonstrated that day along the river, however, the truth never really goes away; it simply waits for the appropriate time to reveal itself.

Since I first heard the story of Woman Who Lived With Wolves, I have learned more and more about wolves. I was especially fascinated with the theme of that first story, never questioning whether it was true. "Why," I asked at some point, "did the wolves help the woman?"

The answer was simple: They made her part of their family.

If we listen to the usual European and Euro-American diatribes about wolves, words like *packs, fangs, vicious,* and *treacherous* are liberally used. The words build barriers made of false impressions, barriers that prevent us from learning the realities about wolves. One of those realities is *family*.

The greatest weakness of humans is arrogance. It blinds us to the realities of other aspects of the world around us. Arrogance tells us that humans are the highest form of life and prompts us to label anything that is like us as "almost human." Such an attitude would cause us to regard the story of Woman Who Lived With Wolves as merely an interesting story, with no possible connection to reality. Yet it is interesting to note that recent scientific studies have revealed that there is indeed a family hierarchy among wolves. That knowledge is regarded as a "discovery" in scientific circles. Among many native peoples who have strong ties to their past, however, that knowledge is as old as time itself.

After my grandfather told me that story, other information about wolves flowed like water. He described how wolves were likely the greatest hunters of all, not because they were physically strong and possessed boundless endurance, which they did. Rather, they were great hunters because they persevered and worked together. They failed more often than they succeeded, but they never quit. Immediately, I wanted to be a wolf because I liked to hunt. But over time, I became more fascinated with another aspect of being a wolf: family.

My grandfather described how the wolves in one group or unit were usually all related by blood or were accepted into the group if they were not related. The family was led by a *bloka*, or "male", and a *winyela*, or "female," labeled the alpha male and female by nonnative observers.

The bloka and winyela had a litter of young usually every year. Those young stayed with the family after they were weaned and grew to young adulthood. So, the core family was several generations of offspring, but only the bloka and the winyela mated and bore young. As the offspring grew into adulthood, they would go off to form their own families. Now and then, lone wolves were allowed to join the family because—as my grandfather pointed out—there were no orphans among wolves.

Some years later, I learned about a ceremony called the *hunka*, known as "making peace" or sometimes "taking as relative." The word comes from *hun*, meaning "mother," and *ka*, meaning "forever." Our word for "mother," *hunkun*, is derived from it; other derivatives are *nihun*, "your mother," and *ina*, the word we use when we address our mothers, not unlike "mom."

The hunka ceremony was primarily to acknowledge *Ina Maka*—or Mother Earth, as it were—signifying that as we make peace, we affirm that no matter how miserable or prosperous we are, Mother Earth will always love us. Therefore, we acknowledge the sacred status of mothers. One of the reasons for doing the hunka ceremony is to take relatives, usually taking someone as son or daughter or mother or father—not unlike wolves who take a stray or lone wolf into the family.

My grandfather, as it turned out, knew much about wolves. In the larger picture, no book I ever read told me anything new or different about wolves that he hadn't mentioned in one way or another. It was his knowledge and his connection to wolves that motivated me to become part of the effort to reintroduce wolves into Yellowstone National Park. In 1991, I became a volunteer for The Wolf Fund, a nonprofit organization that spearheaded that effort. In the autumn of 1995, in spite of spirited efforts by livestock growers near the park, the federal government put wolves back into

Yellowstone (clearly one of the more positive, altruistic acts the government has ever done).

Without a doubt, the centuries-old European and Euro-American fears of and attitudes about wolves still prevail; I call it the "Little Red Riding Hood" syndrome. Recently, there were discussions about reintroducing wolves into the Olympic National Forest on the Olympic Peninsula in Washington State. On the heels of one of the first news stories about that possibility were "anti-wolf" people, who warned that wolves would steal children, as they "always" had in their interrelationship with humans.

My thoughts about wolves, obviously, are different. I don't think of wolves as tireless hunters, although they are. I tend to think of them as the epitome of family. Wolves, as my grandfather pointed out, are the most patient parents on the face of the Earth, and they support and defend their families with all the skills and abilities at their disposal.

My grandparents and wolves have much in common. I know that I tested my grandparents' patience to the limits, but they never stopped loving me or nourishing me in body and spirit. Each and every time I see a picture of a wolf, I think of my grandparents. Anytime I think of my grandparents, the images of the bloka and the winyela rise and take shape in my mind.

Perhaps if we humans could put aside our prejudices and fears about wolves and take onto ourselves the reality of wolves, the world might be a different place. Probably a better place.

As for me, *mayaca*, the wolf, will always mean *family*.

3

The Greyhound

There are many trails on the overall journey that is life, and there are many who travel a trail with us, sometimes briefly. But all the travelers we encounter on our journey have something to teach us.

One such traveler that crossed my path was a dog. Where he came from we never knew, nor do I know where he went after his sojourn with us. But I will never forget him. He was obviously part greyhound, as I look back on it now. I say "part" because his hair was longer than most greyhounds I've seen since.

My grandparents and I had dogs, at least four as I recall. One evening, there was a loud commotion outside among them. My grandfather and I went out to investigate and found the reason: a skinny, gray dog who stood his ground at the edge of the lantern light. In spite of the incessant barking of our dogs, he seemed to be above it all, hardly annoyed by the snarling feints as our two younger dogs rushed at him. Eventually, they settled themselves down when it was apparent the newcomer would not react, or perhaps he was waiting for the right moment to do so. In any case, the commotion ceased, and my grandmother tossed him a scrap of meat. The greyhound delicately picked it up and trotted off into the darkness. I thought he was gone for good, perhaps only searching for a quick handout. But I was wrong. The next morning, he was sitting a stone's throw from our house, waiting.

As the crow flies, we lived seven miles or so from a small town and perhaps two miles west of a north-south highway. So it was anybody's guess as to where the dog had come from. Maybe from a passing vehicle, I thought. He wore no collar, although in the 1950s I can't recall seeing any dog with a collar. He was not the most pleasant-looking dog I had ever seen, so I chose to ignore him. My grandmother, on the other hand, fed him. I thought that the dog decided to stay around for those few scraps, until I saw him catch a rabbit.

My grandfather and I had walked to a long, wide gully that opened onto the floodplain below us so we could pile dry wood for kindling. We noticed that the greyhound was following us, but was keeping a respectful distance.

We finished our chore and were climbing back to the plateau when a jackrabbit exploded from a low thicket and bounded across the prairie. The greyhound flashed past us and the rabbit accelerated, moving faster than I had ever seen any living thing move. It seemed to glide above the grass. Foolish dog, I thought to myself, you will not catch that rabbit.

But I was wrong.

The dog did not actually pursue the jackrabbit. As the rabbit hit top speed, the dog seemed to angle to the left and was soon a gray blur through the grass. My grandfather stopped and shaded his eyes to watch. Jackrabbits, as I learned later, have a peculiar habit of making a wide circle when pursued. No four-legged hunter on the prairie can match their straightaway speed, so the rabbits eventually make a wide turn and end up near the entrance to their den or burrow, having easily outrun any pursuit.

But not, as it turned out, on this particular afternoon.

Off in the distance, perhaps a hundred yards, two gray forms collided, then came a faint squeal, then silence. Apparently, the greyhound had timed his pursuit and hit the jackrabbit in mid-stride, closing in on him at an angle from the left side. The dog had caught himself a sumptuous meal. Although I had seen it happen, I couldn't believe that the greyhound had outsmarted the rabbit. Then he really caught my attention when he dragged the rabbit's carcass across the prairie to our house and shared his food with our dogs.

What, I wondered, was this dog doing here?

Apparently, we were simply a way station along his journey. He stayed with us over the winter until early spring. Then, just as suddenly as he had appeared, he took his leave. I never saw him again.

My grandparents and I talked often of why the greyhound came to our place. A mile to the west of us lived my grandmother's cousin and his family. Further down the river valley was a white rancher, and near the highway was another ranch. But for reasons known only to him, that dog stayed with us over that winter. And a hard winter it was.

The snow came early and filled the gullies and every low spot around. Our horses had to scrounge hard to find grass to graze. Hunting deer that winter was not easy. Perhaps, we thought, the greyhound knew the winter would be hard and simply wanted shelter from the cold and an occasional scrap of food. We were all more than happy to give him both.

Although our dogs stayed together in a small shelter on the lee side of our log house, the greyhound chose to live beneath the woodpile. In the hierarchy of dogs, they seem to acknowledge the strongest in their group, and that was the case after the greyhound took up residence with us. Whether it was the first greeting of the day or after he returned from a hunt, the others licked his face and lay down on their backs in obvious supplication to him. He took all of the posturing in stride with an air of calm dignity, and he never took advantage of his position. He simply accepted it.

Strangely enough, even as the other dogs deferred to him, the greyhound, in turn, deferred to my grandfather. Clearly he was acknowledging the presence of a more dominant being. As I recall, the only time he wagged his tail was whenever my grandmother appeared. He tolerated me with the same parental patience he displayed toward the younger dogs.

Sometime in January, we lost one of our horses. My grandparents owned three large draft horses, part Percheron, I believe. They pulled our wagon and the single-bottom plow. One of the mares, a sorrel named *Hinsmila*, which means "hairy," because she had a long coat all year long, fell into a narrow snow-filled gully and was smothered. Though she died fewer than a hundred yards from our house, the coyotes came and made short work of her carcass. It was a hard winter, after all, and they had to find food where they could. Coyotes are normally wary of humans, but they seemed to get over their fear of us because they came very close to the house one night. A few nights later, they came after our dogs.

Loud snarls and yelps awoke us all one night. My grandfather grabbed his .22-caliber rifle and hurried out into the frigid darkness. He returned shortly to announce that the dogs were safe. The greyhound had attacked the coyotes with such ferocity, although there were four or five of them, that he was able to drive them off. As a precaution, Grandpa brought the dogs inside to spend the night with us. Only the greyhound refused the invitation, choosing instead to retire to his cozy hole beneath the woodpile.

The coyotes stayed away and did not bother our dogs the rest of the winter.

Spring did eventually come. There was one last snowstorm, but thereafter the days were warm, and the snow melted away quickly. We could all see that the greyhound was getting restless.

The rancher who leased some of my grandmother's land brought over part of the lease payment: a yearling steer that we butchered immediately. My grandmother, as was her habit, tossed the scraps to the dogs, but she seemed especially generous to the greyhound. The greyhound enthusiastically accepted her gifts, and gorged himself.

One evening, as my grandparents and I cooked a meal outside after a hard day's work, the greyhound came to us. It was the first and only time he initiated a display of affection, although he had tolerated pats on the head from us now and then. He went first to my grandmother, then to me, and finally to my grandfather. He looked directly into our eyes, each of us in turn. Then he trotted off north across the prairie. We all watched until he disappeared over the edge of the hill that led down into the floodplain.

We never saw him again.

Over the years, we talked about him, speculating on where he might have come from and where he had been going. We lived on that plateau until the following autumn, when we moved into town, but hardly a day passed without a glance toward the horizon to see, perhaps to hope, whether a skinny, gray dog might stop by for a visit. He never did, but in a way he was always part of us.

I can see him still.

There are various bits and pieces of memory regarding that mysterious greyhound. But the one that comes most frequently is the look in his eyes that evening he obviously said good-bye to us. I saw a smile in those light brown eyes, but I also remember sadness behind them. And, for certain, they were the eyes of a gentle soul.

That greyhound had become part of our family for that hard winter, and he still is, in a way. I like to imagine that he and my grandparents have reconnected on the other side. Perhaps my grandparents now know his story.

I know that the greyhound had a particular journey to make. I think he was going home, wherever that was. Though we had given him sustenance and comfort, and he was grateful to us for that, his greater loyalty—and love—he held for someone or something else. I believe in my heart that he finally did make it home. He was too extraordinary a being not to succeed. I can only hope that whoever, or whatever, he loved so much that he was willing to endure hardships for was worth the effort.

There were times I know I crossed some line when I patted his head or scratched his chin. He tolerated those displays of affection aloofly, as if reminding me that *he* was the adult, the elder, and *I* was the child. But whenever I touched him, I felt his strength. Now I know that it was his strength of spirit.

I also recall the various scars on his face and body. He obviously had to defend himself, just as he had defended our dogs against the coyotes. His scars reminded me of something my grandfather liked to say: "Life isn't worth living unless you defend it now and then."

I still wonder, Why did that greyhound come to our place, a log house in the middle of nowhere? Perhaps it was coincidence, but I like to think there was a purpose to it all. Maybe one day I will meet him on the other side, and he can tell me his story. But until then, I think he came to us because he needed us, but he also brought us a gift, especially to me. He taught me never to give up, never to waver from the goal or purpose I see for myself or that life ordains for me.

The plateau where our log house stood is still there. Shortly after we moved, the house was sold and dismantled, and it didn't take the land long to reclaim the old homesite. In the years before my grandfather died, we went back several times. Sometimes the visits were brief, and other times we would spend an entire afternoon or a day. Grandpa liked to walk over the prairie and point out where a trail had once passed. One time he pointed out an old site where his mother-in-law, my great-grandmother, had lived many years before he had built our log house. The land held many memories for both of my grandparents, as it does now for me.

During one of those walks, the year before he died, I could almost see a lifetime of memories playing in his eyes, though he didn't share them with me that day. He simply walked. I think he was saying good-bye because the next journey was waiting for him.

He pointed out to me that there are many trails on the land, some that are so old we can no longer see them or remember exactly where they were. But they are there, he said. He also reminded me that there are trails in our memories; the trails we have walked and the trails left by those who have crossed our paths.

Each and every trail is a story of a journey, he said.

And as he said that, I thought of that skinny greyhound, as I still often do.

4

The Bow and the Arrow

Among other things, my grandfather was a maker of bows and arrows. He couldn't help it, he said, because it was in his blood.

We Lakota are fortunate to have retained as much of our culture as we have. Our language is still alive, as is our kinship system, too. Then there are the songs and dances, not to mention our spiritual beliefs. Yet there are some things we have lost or are in danger of losing, such as the knowledge to make bows and arrows.

I suppose, in the big picture, if we lose the knowledge to make bows and arrows and keep the Seven Sacred Ceremonies brought to us by the White Buffalo Calf Maiden, that is a good trade-off. And only those who know the art of making bows and arrows would be fully aware of what would be lost.

For countless generations, Lakota bows and arrows were the predominant weapon for hunters and warriors. On the one hand, they were nothing more than weapons, but on the other hand they are insights into spirituality. There is obviously more to bows and arrows than the mechanics of making and using them.

Hardwood from oak, ash, and chokecherry trees was used for bows. Arrows were most often made of sandbar willows and young chokecherry saplings. During the winter months, when the sap was down in trees, the bow maker harvested a tree, usually the size of his forearm and as long as he was tall. Winter was also the best time to cut stalks for arrows.

But before the bow maker cut the tree or stalks, he made an offering of tobacco and a prayer of thanksgiving for the life he was about to take. The crafting of a bow or arrow occurred only when the craftsman was in a good frame of mind, when his spirit was balanced and things in his life were generally good. Bows and arrows were never made during periods of difficulty, such as a death in the family. The bow maker believed that his overall frame of mind became part of the bow and arrow. If a bow maker worked on a bow during bad times, it would not be as strong as it could have been and would break easily.

The bow maker also believed that he had taken the life of the bow tree and the arrow stalk before their earthly journey was completed. Therefore, to honor their sacrifice, he was obligated to make the best bow and arrow he could, and applied all of his knowledge, experience, and skill in the process. But his spiritual relationship to the bow and arrow continued after they were finished and he, or someone else, used them on a regular basis.

The bottom of the tree as a bow stave was marked, so was the bottom of the arrow stalk, because as the finished bow and arrow the archer had to keep them in balance with the flow of life upward from the Earth, as they had in life. Interestingly, a bow that was inverted would break easily.

In the act of shooting, the archer would nock (fit) the arrow onto the string by its notch, and then, as he drew (pulled back the string), he would point the tip, or head, of the arrow toward the sky. In doing so, he briefly realigned the arrow with the Earth, because the notch is the bottom of the stalk. This momentary alignment, before he sighted on the target, allowed the power of Mother Earth to empower the arrow. My grandfather reminded me of these truths often, and I can hear him each time I pick up my bow and arrows, even if I'm doing nothing more than practicing.

I am also reminded that the bow and arrow are symbols of the marriage of a man and a woman. In the old days, my grandfather said, a very old and wise man who was a skilled and experienced bow maker was always asked to speak at marriage ceremonies. His purpose was to offer guidance to newlyweds and to give a reminder to those already married.

The message such an old man offered was eloquently simple: Be like the bow and arrow.

Why, then, is that important advice?

There are many realities in life, but the reality of the bow and arrow is that one cannot be fulfilled without the other. Each gives purpose to the other. Without the bow, the arrow cannot fly. Without the arrow, the bow is empty. And there is more.

Every archer knows that no matter how strong a bow may be, the arrow must be perfectly straight in order to fly true to the target. On the other hand, even the straightest arrow cannot reach the target if the bow is weak.

As far as I'm concerned, both sets of my grandparents epitomized the relationship of the bow and arrow. My maternal grandparents were married fifty-five years;

my paternal grandparents were married more than fifty years as well. In each case, my grandmothers outlived my grandfathers, and death was the only thing that separated them in this life.

My grandfather Albert surely would have been that old man invited to speak of the bow and arrow at a marriage ceremony. Not only was he a maker of bows and arrows, he and my grandmother were also the best examples of the allegory. Yet he was never asked to do so, probably because Christianity had taken hold, and I suspect that no Christian minister wanted to hear the philosophy of a culture that Christianity had worked so hard to destroy. Furthermore, if anyone today were to stand and advise a young Lakota couple to "be like the bow and arrow," chances are the advice would be lost on them. It would be lost because the bow and arrow has, for all intents and purposes, fallen by the wayside. Nevertheless, those of us who know anything of the old ways do try to speak of them, because we were told to do just that by those who gave us the knowledge: our parents and grandparents. Furthermore, there are reminders that come from the world around us. Each time I see the thin sliver of a new moon, I am reminded that Lakota bows have been crafted according to that design. That sliver of a new moon is thickest in the middle and tapers gradually to its thinnest point at both ends. In reality, when a bow is constructed in that shape, given that all other rules and processes are followed, it can absorb the stress of being drawn time after time. As any proponent of primitive archery knows, each time a bow is drawn, it is on the way to being broken. The design taken from the moon, or given to us by the moon, is the one that has worked best for us for countless generations.

Likewise, when I see the rays of the sun slicing through the clouds, I am reminded that arrows must be straight as straight can be. As my grandfather said, they must be "straight like the arrows of the sun."

In our culture, we regard the moon as female. It stands to reason then, that the bow is female. The sun is thought of as male, because its power induces Mother Earth to renew life every spring. Therefore, because arrows must be as straight as the rays of the sun, arrows are male. That is precisely why the bow and arrow are the symbols for a good marriage, because one is female and the other is male.

My grandfather talked of such things at practically anytime the inclination came to him. But he did so most often when were out on the land, among the trees, interacting with all the living things that were part of that environment. When we picked chokecherries, for example, he would take the opportunity to teach me that a fully grown chokecherry tree was, in his opinion, the best wood for making a bow, while a young choke-cherry stalk, a sapling, was good for arrows. In the old days, he said, chokecherry arrows were used to hunt bison because they were slender hardwoods and didn't break easily. What's more, they had the weight to penetrate deep into the bison's chest.

If we happened to be near the river and came across a stand of sandbar willows, my grandfather would expound on the qualities that made them the best wood for arrows. Sandbar willow is softwood, and if a stalk was continually straightened as it air-dried, then arrows made from them would stay straight. Arrows made from sandbar willows also flew faster than any other kind.

I never doubted anything my grandfather told me (or anything any of my grandparents told me, for that matter). The realities he taught me about making bows and arrows have proven to be just that time after time. If I failed to mark the bottom of a bow stave and inverted it, thereby keeping it from its natural association with Mother Earth, the finished bow did break, just as he told me it would. All the realities he taught me about the Earth, about life, have all proven themselves time and again. However, the reality he would have me accept about himself was that he was a simple man. But he was far from that; he was many things. No one, man or woman, who has lived a long life should be thought of as simple, no matter how much they insist they are. That insistence is a mark of humility and wisdom. They are humble because they do not take themselves seriously, and they are wise because they want us to think our journey is no less important than theirs was.

Like many of man's institutions and devices, the bow and the arrow has evolved. Now they are of "space age" materials and mass-produced. In the old days, each Lakota man made his own weapons and tools, and every process of handcrafting them was a mechanical as well as a spiritual task. Sadly, that is not the case today. However, there has been a resurgence of interest in what is called "primitive archery." Its participants and practitioners make bows and arrows using only natural materials and hand tools. Logically and unavoidably, many of the primitive bows and arrows are of some indigenous design from North America, and many "primitive archers" emulate a particular indigenous method of shooting.

I am encouraged by this resurgence in primitive archery. If nothing else, the tangible aspects of it will keep the art of making primitive bows and arrows alive. But I wonder if all the modern proponents and practitioners of primitive archery are aware of the intangible aspects of what they have involved themselves with. I truly hope so. The evolution of technology is not automatic affirmation that we, as humans, have also become wiser. We are wiser only if we understand that the past is not passé. We are wiser only if we understand that the tools and the knowledge of our ancestors are the foundation for our evolvement. That kind of insight will enable us to reconnect with our past, our history, and prevent us from being blinded by the modern version of ourselves.

I can count on one hand the number of Lakota people, men or women, who truly know and practice the art of making primitive Lakota bows and arrows. But I am immensely encouraged by the reality that the art is not completely forgotten. My oldest son is learning the art, and my youngest daughter is deeply interested. There is real hope that the knowledge handed down by my grandfather will survive at least another generation beyond mine. I'm sure that is precisely what he thought.

Thanks to my grandfather, I am a maker of bows and arrows. Both the process and the finished product connect me to the past, a connection that reaches back across time, across more generations than I will ever know. And that connection is really the trail that my grandfather has enabled me to walk. Though I followed him along the tangible trails that crisscrossed the land, he was really leading me back toward his parents' and grandparents' world, and to their parents and grandparents, and so on. Thanks to his vivid descriptions, I can see that world, and to a certain extent, I can re-create it if I choose to. There are moments, when the sound and the fury of our times seem to fly at me from every direction, that I yearn for a different world and the times my grandfather taught me about. Yet he also taught me that I have to walk forward into the future, just as he and my grandmother had to do, and as their parents and grandparents had to do.

And so I will, as a maker of bows and arrows.

5

The Shadow Man

Wars and warriors invariably become part of a young boy's imagination, especially after hearing stories of heroes like Crazy Horse of the Oglala Lakota and Spotted Tail, a Sicangu Lakota. Both became *naca*, overall leaders of their respective bands, but both had been exemplary fighting men as well. Those were the heroes most boys aspired to when playing at war. In Lakota culture, such play and the games of war are intended to teach the skills necessary to fight an enemy. They also help awaken something inside the boy.

I can't recall the precise moment the question arose in my mind, but I think it was prompted by two seemingly unrelated events. In a seventh-grade history class, a non-Indian teacher had talked at length about Indian "braves" going on the "warpath." Sometime later, while walking across a meadow with my grandfather, we saw a badger chase a coyote away from the mouth of its hillside den. Something about that incident prompted me to ask my grandfather what the word for "war" was in Lakota. After a thoughtful moment or two, he concluded that although there was a word for "fighting," *wicakizapi,* and "battle," *wicokize,* he could think of no word that encompassed the broader meaning of the English word war.

That particular moment has risen to the top of my pile of boyhood memories more than many others. At the very least, probably because I am now more aware that cultural definitions of the same word, especially those representing more abstract things, often point to philosophical variances rather than semantic nuances.

For example, the Lakota word *akicita* has come to mean "soldier." Its original meaning was to denote the members of "warrior societies," or *akicita omniciye.* Thus, in the rationale applied by non-Indian linguists, *akicita* was the Lakota word for "warrior," a seemingly logical assumption. However, as my grandfather pointed out, the phrases *zuya ye* and *zuya mani* meant "going to battle" and "walking to battle." Colloquially, then, the phrases meant "going off to war." *Zuya wicasa* meant "man who battles" or "man who goes to battle" and later was deemed comparable to the English word "warrior." Today, anyone who has served in the modern military is described as *akicita opa*, meaning he or she "was a member of the soldiers," no matter what branch of service he or she served in.

I concluded later that the label "warpath" was the Euro-American society's attempt to describe an aspect of Lakota culture. Likewise, the word "brave" was an ethnocentric, perhaps even a racist, label for native fighting men, a jibe at a culture considered quaint and inferior.

The unavoidable fact was that warfare and "going to battle" were necessary parts of the Lakota lifestyle, especially after contact with Euro-Americans. The nomadic hunting lifestyle necessarily meant that the male fulfilled the societal role as a provider, or the hunter—*waye wicasa* or *wakuwa*. The other part of a male's societal role was as the *zuya wicasa*, the "man who goes to battle." Overall, the male was the *hunter/warrior*.

One day, still somewhat confused by the seemingly convoluted labels, I asked my grandfather for some kind of clarification. Consequently, he brought up an entirely different phrase and its concept: *nagi wica*, or "shadow man." He expounded at some length on the issues of war and warriors. His explanation was a foundation for insights I am still developing over this most chaotic of human institutions, and of understanding those who are thrust into war or go by choice.

In my grandfather's opinion, war is really a fight between the good and the bad sides of humans, and both emerge during hostilities. It is within each of us to bring out the best or the worst part of ourselves. In all endeavors, he said, we must strive for balance, even within the context of war.

As a student and young adult, I was frequently subjected to the Euro-American sociological and anthropological assessments of native societies. Numerous books talked about "warlike" Indians and said that Plains peoples were so warlike that they "lived for war," in the words of one Cheyenne warrior. War, in the opinion of many Euro-American anthropologists, gave meaning and definition to the existence of Plains tribes. It behooves us to consider, however, that the opinion of even the most learned and well-meaning non-Indian anthropologist is not totally objective.

I recall the anecdote told to me by a Lakota elder regarding the word *Wakantanka*. He gave that word when a non-Indian researcher asked him to say the Lakota word for *God*. *Wakantanka* means "holy" or "sacred" and "great or powerful beyond description." It is often translated as the "Great Mystery." All of these translations apply, because to us there is no one easy way to describe God, and all of them are equivalent to the Christian concept of what God is. When the elder explained all of that, the researcher then replied, "Okay, but what does it really mean?"

Although I understand that one needs a point of reference to make comparisons, I do firmly believe that anthropologists, and any non-Indian who seeks information about native cultures and societies, cannot be truly objective. They form opinions based on comparisons with their own cultural and societal information and present them as fact or reality. In other words, the "facts" they uncover about any aspect of native culture is tainted by the inherent, ethnocentric notion that who and what they are culturally—as researchers and observers—is better than what they are observing. That goes hand-in-hand with the equally common mind-set that if one culture behaves in one way, then all cultures do. Thus, I believe that European and Euro-American observers of native cultures and societies assume that North American natives have the same bent for imperialistic warfare that Europeans did and do have. That, then, is likely the basis for the assumption that North America was a continuous hotbed of all-out warfare among native tribes. When such conclusions are drawn by established non-Indian scholars, with all the appropriate credentials, any counterpoint by natives who know their own culture and history is dismissed.

But the fact is that pre-European North America was not a constant battleground or killing field. There were conflicts, to be sure, but not on the scale assumed by Europeans and Euro-Americans. As far as numbers and frequency are concerned, warfare on a scale comparable with that in Europe simply didn't happen. As a matter of fact, many native peoples of the Plains found it difficult to believe that often tens of thousands of soldiers could be killed in just *one* battle during the Civil War. It was not only the numbers that were unbelievable, but also the idea that *killing* and *destruction* were the way the whites waged war. The native people of the Plains were equally incredulous to learn that soldiers were *paid* to wage war, to kill and destroy.

Yet there was a valid reason that all males in Lakota culture fulfilled the dual role of provider and protector—the hunter/warrior, as it were. Both roles had the same general objective. One provided the necessities for survival by making food, shelter, and clothing available. The other protected the ability to thrive.

The words of a song honoring fighting men sum up the societal attitude toward the calling to be the protector:

I go forward under the banner of the people.

I do this so that the people may live.

There was no higher calling than to defend the people—it was a lifelong obligation for all males. Thus, to "go to battle" in the name of and on behalf of the people was both a practical necessity and a patriotic duty.

Unlike Euro-American society, the Lakota did not pay their fighting men to kill and conquer in their name. Yet, there was a payoff: Warfare was a proving ground. Combat offered males the opportunity to demonstrate courage. Because of the obvious danger to life and limb, the most courageous act was to touch a live enemy during combat. Enough such courageous deeds defeated the enemy's spirit, or his will to fight, thus demonstrating that killing was not always the means to victory.

Whatever the reason for "going to battle," combat—to say the least—is not a pleasant activity. But it did and does occur; it continues to be part of the interaction between human nations and societies the world over. No one, no matter how justified, imperialistic, or mean-spirited, participates in it willingly. There is always part of the spirit or the mind, or both, that is reluctant. What then enables people to participate in combat, despite that reluctance?

The answer is the *Shadow Man*, or *Shadow Woman*, as the case may be.

That *shadow being* lives within each of us. He or she is the one that pushes back when someone pushes us. It is, as the label implies, the dark side of each of us. Its strengths are anger, recklessness, and impulsiveness, and most of its existence (in most cases) is spent waiting to emerge. Adversity most often pulls the shadow being from its dormancy, where it is held in abeyance by the absence of conflict. A threat to or an attack on family and community or self is the most common call to arms for the shadow being. When it emerges, there is no hesitancy, no tentativeness.

When it does emerge, its only limitation is the character of our overall being and the values and morals that we live by. If our character and values and morals are strong, then when the shadow being's purpose is served, we can return it to the shadows to wait once more. If we can't return it to the shadows, it will run amok. A young Marine lieutenant, a leader of a rifle platoon in Vietnam, was appalled when one of his men tied a string of human ears to his belt, grisly trophies taken from enemy dead. Without a moment's hesitation, the lieutenant ordered the young private to burn the ears and bury the ashes, then he oversaw the task to ensure that his orders were carried out—in full view of the entire platoon. Clearly he was making certain that the shadow man was not given the opportunity to run amok.

My grandfather reminded me that the honoring songs sung to and about warriors were really to remind the shadow man that he does have a higher purpose, even though, at times, he must employ dark actions to achieve it.

Among several Plains tribes, such as the Lakota, there was a cleansing and healing ceremony for fighting men. Those who had participated in battle, or battles, were placed outside the circle of the community; a dance arbor represented that circle as the people stood within it. Songs were sung to honor the fighting men, and prayers were offered for their souls so that they be cleansed of the terrible things they had to do to defend the people. Then the men walked quietly back into the circle, back into the community, because the people allowed them to return so that they could be healed. Not only were the men, in a sense, forgiven for being warriors, but they were also reminded that the *nagi wica* was to be put back in its state of dormancy each time it fulfilled its purpose. It was a reality check to remind them, in no uncertain terms, that though there was honor and status to be won as fighting men, that was only part of their responsibility to the community.

As the community reminded the men that their overall responsibility was broader than their obligation as protectors, it—the community made up of wives, mothers, fathers, children, and grandparents—was also healing emotional, as well as physical, wounds suffered in defense of the people. Any society, any culture, any community that—as a whole—unconditionally heals and nurtures its warriors is ensuring its own survival. Any society, culture, or community that does so understands that being a warrior is much more than a job or a career. It is a calling, a sacred duty that is carried out when necessary. Such a society knows and understands the shadow being.

The shadow being does live within each of us, waiting for that necessary moment to emerge. We can see it emerge when a mother fiercely or steadfastly defends her children from any kind of harm. At such moments, the shadow being becomes the one who "goes to battle," or *zuya ye*, and in a real sense becomes the "warrior."

Sadly, war will not cease to be, at least not in the foreseeable future. Neither will conflicts within our everyday lives. Consequently, war and warriors will continue to be a fabric of the lore of many cultures the world over, no matter the cause. Therefore, the shadow being will continue to be part of us, individually and collectively.

Perhaps a way to eradicate war and to understand the shadow being is to forgive the warriors so they can forgive themselves and heal, especially from the wounds that are hardest to see—the wounds to the soul. Then perhaps we can all understand what my grandfather said to me: The real warrior is the one who fights to defeat war itself.

6

Follow Me

Whenever my grandfather and I took walks, especially when I was still a boy, he always led the way. He led the way because he knew the trails well in all seasons of the year. Winter trails were different from summer trails. Gentle slopes easily traversed in the summer turned slippery and dangerous with winter snows. Yet in the winter, we could walk over the very spots where rattlesnakes were likely to hide in the summer. There is something to be said for heading into unexplored territory, but there is also something to be said for knowing where you are going. The latter, I believe, is a mark of a good leader.

For the pre-reservation Lakota, good leadership was essential to survival, and one critical requirement for leadership was experience. The overall leadership for a given community or group was the council of elders, simply because they had experienced life. They could therefore bring the weight and the strength of those experiences—failures as well as successes—to bear on any question or issue brought before them.

There were military and civilian leaders, of course, who were responsible for facing and mitigating threats to overall welfare and meeting day-to-day needs. They were selected not only on the basis of their character and ability but also on the level of their experience. Development and selection of leaders was a significant part of Lakota culture, and each aspect was based on common sense and practicality.

The axiom "Whatever doesn't kill you will make you stronger" cuts across many cultural lines and sheds a great deal of light on the development of leaders in Lakota culture of old. Difficulty is one of the best builders of character, and one of the most difficult arenas to prove oneself was in combat. Though the Lakota probably didn't start fights for the sake of creating a difficult situation in which to place young men, combat and warfare were nonetheless a logical proving ground. If a man could consistently display calmness, good judgment, and courage within that very difficult circumstance, he could likely apply the same virtues in the time of peace. Anyone who did so acquired a following as a combat or war leader and was considered a good prospect as a civilian leader. Therefore, warrior societies and the community at large kept a close eye on up-and-coming young men.

The people selected their leaders, but they didn't pick from a slate of candidates who stood for election. There was no election process at all. The people simply approached the man they felt was the right choice; and that man had the prerogative to say "yes" or "no." Interestingly, many of the men approached for leadership were reluctant to take on the responsibility. More often than not, those men who hesitated made the best leaders. Once a man accepted a leadership position, there were no prescribed terms of office, as it were. As long as a man exercised good judgment, made good decisions, and took responsibility for his actions, people would follow him. If a man did none of those things or was more interested in the glory and fame of leadership, the people turned away and no longer followed. In other words, the people had the last word in the selection and retention of leaders. They were not forced to follow a bad leader because his term of office had not expired.

Good leaders and good leadership are essential for any society to survive and thrive. Interestingly, however, and perhaps even sadly, leadership has become synonymous with authority. Therefore, the power of the office occupied by today's leaders is often more important than character and experience. Consequently, a leader sometimes does something because he or she can, not because it is necessarily the right thing to do.

Although a simplistic, and perhaps idealistic, way to look at leaders is to determine whether they "lead the way" or "point the way," it is also a very elemental and practical way to assess leaders and their leadership. In other words, does a leader say "Follow me," or does he or she say "Do as I say and not as I do"?

A leader who leads the way, figuratively or realistically, is one who understands that character and experience are more important than authority and that actions speak louder than words. Authority is obviously built into the framework of leadership in this day and age, but that doesn't necessarily have to be the sole basis from which a leader operates. The application of character and experience into leadership decisions can enhance authority. But decisions based consistently on authority will create a dependency on authority and will, over time, eliminate the application of character and experience.

The values he learned as a boy, primarily from his immediate family and personal mentors, taught the Oglala Lakota leader Crazy Horse that it was necessary to provide for those who were in need, especially the elderly. As a teenager, he demonstrated the virtue of compassion and exercised the qualities of a leader, whether or not he realized it. He hunted and brought back fresh meat for those families who had no one to provide for them. In doing so, he showed what others could do for those in need, and he did it without saying a word.

Leadership by example, in my opinion, is the most effective kind.

Being mayor or governor or president doesn't mean one automatically becomes a leader in the true sense of the word. To be sure, we sometimes do have mayors and governors and even presidents who are good and effective leaders. But, by and large, we are more often saddled with politicians and authoritarians who grow up "dreaming of becoming president" and who do not remotely understand that a true leader must often sacrifice ego and personal glory for the sake of those he or she leads.

In May of 1877, nearly a year after the great victory at the Little Bighorn, Crazy Horse surrendered to white authority at Fort Robinson in Nebraska Territory.

There were simply no resources on which to live as his people had for countless generations. The buffalo were gone, slaughtered by white hunters for their hides and tongues. Even if Crazy Horse's band of some 900 people, mostly women and children, could live by hunting, the U.S. government was actively hunting them. Lakota emissaries who were already reservation Indians, some of them old friends of Crazy Horse and some of them his old enemies, were sent by General George Crook to convince the last wild and free band of Lakota to surrender.

For all of his adult life, Crazy Horse had mightily resisted the white man. To surrender to them and live under their control was a sickening prospect. But if he was anything, Crazy Horse was a realist. He was a selfless leader as well. As a realist, he knew that there were so many more white men than there were Lakota, and the white men had more guns and bullets. Crazy Horse's men had to scrounge for bullets. Whatever they had could be expended in one short battle, while the white soldiers had a seemingly endless supply. As a leader, he knew had two choices: continue to fight and risk having all of his followers killed or surrender. In the end, his selflessness motivated him to choose surrender.

When he and his followers arrived at Fort Robinson in May 1877, Crazy Horse was the first to give up his horse and his gun—the very symbols of his warrior life and persona. We can't know exactly how he must have felt at the moment he gave the reins of his horse to a soldier and handed over his rifle, but it had to have been one of the most difficult—if not the most difficult—acts he ever did in his life. We do know this: He had to do it. It wouldn't have been right for him to simply *tell* his 120 warriors to lay down their arms. He had to lead the way, just as he had been doing for nearly twenty years as a warrior and leader. His leadership under those most galling and difficult of moments gave courage to the 900 people who followed him into an uncertain future. That one example—among so very many—stands as the lasting symbol of the kind of leader Crazy Horse was, and that leadership by example, under the best or worst of circumstances, is extremely powerful. That one example is still an inspiration for we Lakota who are aware of our history and Crazy Horse's place in it.

Leadership for and among the Lakota changed, especially after the death of Crazy Horse in 1877 and of Sitting Bull in 1890. After the end of the so-called Indian wars, the various Lakota bands lived virtually under martial law because of the strict control of the U.S. government. The ultimate authority was the Indian Agent (later called a Superintendent), who was the chief administrator at each agency or reservation. In 1934, the U.S. Congress passed the Indian Reorganization Act, ostensibly giving native tribes the right to self-government. The act mandated a legislature form of government for tribes, with a tribal council and an executive branch headed by a president or chairman. I believe that two factors that were part of the mandate have been the main reasons for the deterioration of traditional Lakota leadership.

First, though tribal council could enact legislation (in the form of resolutions), their actions had to be approved by the Indian Agent, and then sent up through the Bureau of Indian Affairs and the federal Department of the Interior for subsequent approval. Tribal council resolutions could be altered at any step before final approval was granted, and only after that approval was a resolution in force.

Second, the minimum age at which a tribal member could stand for election to the council was twenty-five. It might have seemed like a good idea to involve younger people in the governmental process. However, that minimum age requirement effectively undermined the ancient tradition of village councils composed of elders.

Leadership was placed in the hands of the inexperienced, and, consequently, tribal councils have been mired in the same kinds of political problems known to state legislatures and the Congress: factionalism, mud-slinging, influence-peddling, and inconsistency. Leadership is now based on who you know, not what you know.

Good leadership is essential in all walks of life and in every kind of organization. Good leadership, as I see it, is showing the way. Perhaps the best analogy in this day and age is sports teams. Coaches and managers can have the best game plan in the world, but unless the players execute the plan, there is no hope of winning the contest. Invariably, if at least one player performs steadily or spectacularly, those actions speak louder than the words of the coach. The player has exercised leadership more effectively than the coach or manager has because he or she showed the way by the deed, rather than by the word. Leadership by example is still the most effective kind.

I still follow my grandfather. He left many trails across the prairies of my boyhood. I follow him not only because of the trails he left, but more so because of how he walked them and because he knew where he was going. Because he did know where he was going, he could show me the way—and he still does.

7

The Circle of Life

Somewhere along the bottoms near the Little White River, where many of the important adventures of my boyhood seemed to occur, my grandfather tossed a stone into a shallow slough filled with rainwater. Then he pointed to the circles of low waves pushing outward from where the stone had splashed. Those growing circles were my first lesson in spirituality.

The circle, my grandfather explained, is a basic reality of life. The waves in the water do not emanate out in squares or any other shapes, he pointed out. That is one of the most compelling and irrefutable statements I have ever heard in my life.

The shape of the sun and moon is circular, he went on to say. Rainbows are circles, even though we can only see half of them at the most, except when they appear around the sun or moon. The Earth we live on is round, and it leads us to believe that the sun and moon move in a circle around us. Even some illusions are circular.

There are many supporting arguments for the reality of the circle, such as hurricanes and tornadoes. And when a leaf falls from a tree, it spirals, which is a circle.

Over the years, I've found nothing—not that I was trying—to refute the reality of the circle, although I've noticed plenty of affirmations of it. For example, when groups of natives (Indians) gather together, they invariably form a circle. A man wandering in a vast wilderness on foot will eventually walk a circle, because one leg is shorter than the other; therefore, his steps are not equal in length.

It is only fitting, therefore, that the circle is the basis for Lakota spirituality. It is, in fact, the symbol representing life. The physical essence of the circle becomes somewhat abstract as it turns into a *cycle*. Days cycle from darkness to dawn to daylight to dusk and then back to darkness. Seasons of the year cycle from spring to summer to autumn to winter. Our lives cycle from birth to childhood to adulthood to old age and then to death.

Another reality I've discovered since my childhood is that there is no word in English to describe the Lakota belief system. The word *spiritual* separates the physical from what many non-Lakota consider the spirit or soul. According to *Webster's College Dictionary*, *religion* is defined as "a set of beliefs concerning the cause, nature, and purpose of the universe, especially when considered as the creation of a superhuman agency or agencies, usually involving devotional and ritual observances, and often containing a moral code for the conduct of human affairs." This definition, I suppose, comes closest to the Lakota belief system, but it doesn't seem to touch on a word in our language that describes life: *skan* (pronounced shkahn). It is the pronunciation, or *skanskan*, which means "to move" or "to be in motion." It can also mean "the life force" or "everything that moves."

What, I must ask, doesn't move or hasn't moved at one time or another?

I can't look at the circle and not think of motion. Perhaps someone in some bygone age had the same reaction and decided that it represented life. What goes around comes around. It's what a circle does. Perhaps that is why traditional Lakota are not good at linear thinking, but we seem to be able to realize that all things are connected. That idea, to me, is Lakota spirituality.

My grandfather pointed at the emanating waves in the pond and said that it is impossible for one part of the circle to be first or last. This idea was another layer of reality, if you will, about the circle. But that reality is often overlooked, ignored, or simply not understood by Western societies—especially American society.

We human beings, by and large, regard ourselves as the superior form of life on this Earth. We have certainly affected, largely negatively, all other forms of life and the environment itself. Our attitudes and our populations, more than any factors, have had an impact. Simply and tragically, we stop at nothing to change or use the environment to fit our needs. And the more there are of us, the greater the impact.

We tend to think we have "progressed" beyond the "archaic" philosophies of our predecessors regarding anything. But the one area in which this attitude is most damaging is the overblown idea of our place in the physical environment. Western societies, where Christianity is a significant factor, believe that man, or humans, were given "dominion" over the Earth and all other creatures. But that sense of "dominion" certainly hasn't translated into a sense of responsible stewardship. Here is an area where the reality of the circle is sorely needed.

In the circle, there is no first or last, no higher or lower. Many native cultures, the Lakota included, accepted the reality that all forms of life have a place on that circle. Therefore, no one or no thing is first or last. No one or no thing is higher or lower than any other form of life. To further affirm this reality, the irrefutable equalizers are life and death.

The fact is that we are all born and we all die. The connotation "we" goes beyond the narrow anthropocentric viewpoint to include everything, *all* forms of life. No thing or no one lives forever, including humans. Instead of embracing this reality, we humans do everything we can to fight death. It would seem we are in constant denial of it. That is the real reason we build marble crypts and mausoleums. We tell ourselves that we are honoring the life and memory of a loved one, but in truth we are denying the reality of death for as long as possible. By denying death, we are really denying life. Our mortal remains cannot return to the Earth and become the organic material on which other life forms will derive sustenance. That reality is too horrible for most of us to accept.

One of my maternal great-grandfathers was a *wapiya wicasa*, a healer, more commonly referred to as a "medicine man." He died relatively young, at age forty-nine, as the result of an accident. He left instructions, years before he died, that he did not want to be buried in a casket of any kind. So my great-grandmother and his relatives wrapped him in robes and blankets and buried him on a hillside overlooking a river. His body has long since returned to the Earth and has rejoined the circle of life. Thus, for the past ninety-four years, he has lived again and again with each year's growth of grasses on that hillside.

The acceptance of such simple reality is beneath most people, because we tend to regard ourselves as apart from all other species in the world. When we talk about animals, we exclude ourselves from that category. In fact, we are fond of saying that someone behaved "like an animal" when describing behavior that is cruel, chaotic, or senseless. Such sentiments would apply only if we, as a species, never ever—individually or collectively—committed any act that was cruel or chaotic or senseless. Although we have, too many times, we still continue to think we are the epitome of civilized or charitable behavior or thinking or that we are the only species capable of compassion.

Recently, a wealthy businessman bought a special license to hunt bison (buffalo) on an Indian reservation on the northern Plains. His guides escorted him to a pasture where bison were grazing, so there was actually no hunt in the strictest definition of the word. He did not find his prey by the means of fair chase. Nonetheless, he shot one of the bison in the herd with his large caliber rifle. What happened next astounded him. The bison the man had shot and only wounded fell where she stood; the rest of the small herd gathered around her. They stayed with her, obviously agitated at what had occurred, emitting sad, plaintive bleats.

Without a doubt, there are many such lessons all around us, and they probably occur with some regularity. All we need to do is see them and understand the profound reality they offer. The man who killed the bison, although astonished at the behavior of the other members of his victim's herd, called it nothing more than a "curiosity."

Man has an equal place on the circle of life. That doesn't lessen him or exalt others. It is simply a reality. Man, like all creatures, has one ability or characteristic that is his key to survival. Some other animals have speed or the ability to blend in with their environment or some kind of defensive mechanism that effectively prevents a predator from taking its life. We humans have the ability to reason. That's not to say that other animals do not reason. But the ability to reason combined with the development of language has made us a force to be reckoned with. And the Earth has been attempting to reckon with us for a very long time.

Man has turned his greatest strength into his greatest weakness. Our ability to reason has seduced us into thinking we are *the* superior form of life on the planet. We have developed tools and attitudes that enable us to alter the physical environment to suit us, and, consequently, we regard the Earth, and all others who dwell on it with us, as inferior. We continue to attempt to separate ourselves from the circle of life, but we haven't changed the reality of the circle. We don't realize that we are no more or no less than any other form of life. We have failed to realize that our ability to reason has not given us special status, only a greater responsibility. Thus far, we have not honored that responsibility, and that is our weakness. That weakness is a threat to everything and every one who dwells with us on this planet.

In spite of our so-called superiority, we share the same cycle of life with other forms of life. We are born, we live our lives, and we die. Our powerful intellect has not enabled us to alter the cycle. We may be able to manipulate the creation of life, but we haven't altered the reality of birth. We may be able to manufacture good health and circumvent some physical defects with eyeglasses and wheelchairs, for example, but we have not been able to change the inevitability of death.

Political, financial, and even religious power will not save us from death. As a matter of fact, we have not yet evolved spiritually to realize that we do not need to be saved from death. From diseases, discomfort, and a host of other ills, yes. But not from death.

As my grandfather reminded me often, the circle is life. It has no beginning and no ending. Though many of us tend to think that our lives—our journey on this physical plane—ends with death, it is really another beginning. That is the reality of the circle. That is the reality of knowing what true spirituality is. But unless we learn and accept that another kind of life begins with death, we fall short of learning spirituality.

I was a young adult, only in the beginning phases of my journey, when I began to realize that my grandparents, indeed all of them, did not fear death. They feared ill health and frailty, but they understood that those were often conditions of old age. All of them spoke of death often, as if they were conversing about the neighbor down the street. They accepted the inevitable, but they did not resign themselves to it. They accepted death because they knew it was part of reality, and they embraced that reality because they had reached a place in their minds and spirits that gave them a perspective—an illumination, if you will—we all can achieve one day. But just because we can, does not necessarily mean all of us will.

One of the keys to achieving that illumination is to understand the circle. It has no beginning and no end, and there is no part of it that is farther from or closer to the center. So anyone or anything that is on that circle is equal to all others who are there. We human beings have turned away from that reality and have created the illusion that we are superior.

Perhaps, as my grandfather liked to do, we should toss a few stones into a pond and watch the circles it creates.

8

The End of the Journey
Is the Beginning

I can't recall the exact moment when I noticed that my grandfather could not walk as fast or as vigorously as he once had. The silvery-gray hairs on his head seemed a normal part of his appearance until I realized they had not always been there. My grandmother was showing signs of her age, too. Suddenly, it seemed, there were lines on her face and rising out of a chair became more and more difficult for her.

Like anyone, I never imagined my world without my grandparents in it. They had always been there, and part of me assumed—or hoped—they would always be there. But part of me also realized that one day they would be gone. Strangely, however, that realization didn't happen suddenly. It wasn't a thunderclap of a moment that took my breath away. It was, instead, a quiet acceptance of a reality they had not been hesitant or afraid to teach me. There was sadness, to be sure, but because they had not hidden the reality of the cycle of life from me, they gave me the insight and the strength to cope with it.

At some point, we had moved from the log house on the prairie into town, a small town where I went to school. School was only a few blocks away, as was the grocery store. My grandparents didn't drive, so in town we walked everywhere. Sometimes in the summers, we walked to church, five miles from town. My grandmother was a devout Episcopalian. I can recall many a Sunday morning when we would start walking very early along the main highway to the south. Amazingly, never did we have to walk the entire five miles. Somehow we were always able to catch a ride and get to church on time. Many times we were the first to arrive, and always someone would give us a lift back to town. Eventually that little country church was torn down and a new one built in town. But, of course, my grandparents still walked to Sunday service frequently.

We moved to town because it was necessary. My grandfather sold his team of draft horses and the wagon, and the log house as well. I can recall the morning the white rancher who leased my grandmother's land came to take the horses. It was very early in the morning and a commotion awakened me. By the time I looked out the front door, the horses were already loaded in a truck and slowly driving out of our pasture. Deep inside, I knew the moment had been coming, but it was a shock nonetheless. Later, another rancher who had bought the house dismantled it and hauled it away. But we weren't there to see that happen because we were already living in town.

There were to be many changes in my life. By the time I graduated from high school, I had changed schools at least half a dozen times. During some of those years, I lived with my parents, and my father was always looking for the right kind of a job to support a large family of eleven children. He was an automobile mechanic. Moving frequently was hard for all of us, especially changing schools so often, including a few times into communities where we were the only native family and my siblings and I were the only native kids in the school. But part of me did cope, because my grandparents had taught me, taught us all, that change—whether unforeseen, unwanted, or planned—was part of life.

So when that moment of realization came, when I knew that my grandparents were nearing the end of their lives, I also realized they had been preparing me, and all of us, for the one change that would affect us all profoundly.

My paternal grandfather died on December 27, 1974, and my maternal grandfather only a few months later, on March 4, 1975. It was a difficult time for both sides of the family, but it was also a time of reflection for many of us. Both grandfathers had lived well into their eighties and were deeply respected by anyone who knew them, both Indian and white. To this day, I think of them often, and in my mind, they are the Fisherman and the Pipe Maker.

My paternal grandfather, Charles J. Marshall, was an ordained Episcopalian deacon and an avid fisherman. After he retired from the active ministry, he traveled across the state pursuing his love of fishing. My maternal grandfather, Albert Two Hawk, the one who helped raise me, made traditional Lakota pipes from shale and red pipe stone. There was much more to the two men than fishing and pipes, of course, but I can't look at anything connected to fishing without thinking of Grandpa Charlie, and one of the last pipes Grandpa Albert made sits on my fireplace mantle.

Both of my grandmothers were widows for many years. My paternal grandmother, M. Blanche Roubideaux

Marshall, left us on June 11, 1982—the same day one of my daughters was born. I like to think they met in passing. My maternal grandmother, Annie Good Voice Eagle Two Hawk, died in May 1984. Both of them were the epitome of quiet strength and were the focal point of their families.

My father died five years ago of colon cancer. He had been diagnosed too late, and all the treatments and prayers could not save him. But he faced the terribly debilitating and painful disease with grace and courage and left behind a shining example for all of us to follow and remember him by. He also kept the last promise he made to my mother. He promised he would make it to their anniversary, even as the disease weakened him day by day. He died at four in the morning, April 14, the day of their fifty-seventh wedding anniversary. The last voice he heard in this world was my mother's. "Happy anniversary," she told him, a few seconds after midnight. "I love you." He opened his eyes briefly and nodded ever so slightly.

Death comes. Too often it comes tragically. My maternal grandparents lost two sons, one while still a toddler and the other in World War II. One of my aunts, my father's old sister, lost two sons in the same car crash less than a year ago. My sister and one of our cousins each lost a teenage child to car crashes. My uncle lost a daughter and then his wife to cancer. The list goes on. Even when death occurs more or less naturally at the end of a long life, we don't grieve and mourn any less. But part of the coping process is in accepting the reality that death, however it comes, is a part of life.

I can recall asking my grandfather about death, when I was still a boy. I was curious about what happens to us after we die. "We find another place to live" was his reply. Then he touched my head and my chest over my heart. "Here and here," he said. "That is where we will live next." Indeed. In my mind and in my heart is where all my grandparents are, as are friends and relatives who have finished their journeys in this world.

There are moments when the world seems lacking because my grandparents aren't here any longer. But then I remember that they are not gone from it so long as their children and grandchildren remember them. And we do, and so they are still here within us all.

Hours after we buried my father, my mother and my siblings gathered in her house, along with a few dozen grandchildren. Soon and naturally enough, the conversation turned to my father. We reminisced about his life and told stories. All of us had at least one anecdote to share. Some of the stories were about special moments that we had shared, but many of them were also funny. So, for a few hours we laughed, sometimes uproariously. In a very real way, we were sending our father onto his next journey with very good thoughts and with immeasurable love. It was also what we had done for our grandparents.

Death has taken them all, and it will take us, too. But my father and all of my grandparents still live on in our minds and hearts. Their values, their words, habits, mannerisms, failures, and accomplishments. The essence of what they were still lives. Somehow, because of that, their transition to and continuing journey in the next life is easier for them. Perhaps we'll talk about that when we see them again.

As an adult, I took my grandfather to the confluence of the Smoking Earth (Little White) and White Earth (Big White) Rivers, in the northern part of the reservation. There we stopped for a time and walked about. He pointed out an area a few hundred yards from where the Smoking Earth River flowed into the White Earth. He had been born there, he said. It was where his Earthly journey had begun. Less than two years later, he began his journey into the spirit world. Now we take walks in my memory, just as he said we would. Those walks are as meaningful as when they first happened, because he didn't teach me how to deny or conquer death, just simply to take it in stride.

The Wisdom Within

Our journey toward wisdom begins the moment we are born. Everything and everyone around us builds the foundation for what we will be, who we will become, and how we will interact with the things and beings that will be part of that journey.

My playground as a child was 150 square miles of rolling prairies and river valleys in the northern part of the Rosebud Sioux Indian Reservation. It was also a proving ground. The land and my grandparents molded me into the kind of person I am today. And I'm still a work in progress as I embark on my seventh decade.

Many, many trails crisscross those prairies and valleys, and I've lost count of how many of them my grandfather and I walked together. Every walk was an adventure, and every trail led somewhere. Where each and every trail ultimately takes us is up to us, because all trails are choices we make, intentionally or unintentionally. Each and every experience that occurs, and the consequences we suffer or the rewards we reap, shape us into who and what we are.

"You can think whatever you want, say whatever you want, and do whatever you want, as long as you are willing to face the consequences." That was my grandfather's answer on so many occasions when I asked for guidance. It always made me stop to think, to rely on my own instincts, and to consider all the factors in a given situation. The process didn't always guarantee that I would make the right choice or find the right answer, because it wasn't supposed to. It was intended to teach me to live my own life and learn from the good and bad choices.

As a child, I sensed that my grandparents knew a lot. It seemed to me that there was practically nothing they could not do, and they had answers to every question I asked. Therefore, when I faced the first important decision (at least to me) in my life, my grandfather seemed to sidestep the situation with his answer, and I was slightly confused. He would frequently talk in generalities about right or wrong, or about thinking long and hard about a given situation, or about common sense. But he never said "You should do this." After hearing the same answer several times, I wondered if he really cared about me. Now I can understand how hard it was for him to tell me "You can think whatever you what." Parents want to do and be everything for their children, especially prevent them from getting hurt in any way. Both my grandparents were no different in that respect. Because I now have children and grandchildren, I know it wasn't easy for my grandfather to allow me to make my own choices, because he knew that some of them would be wrong. But because he let me live my own life, as it were, and make my own choices, the lessons I learned were also my own and they were and are the basis for wisdom.

When I was about six or seven, I watched my grandfather handcraft a bow. He began with an ash stave nearly six feet long. It had been dried and cured for several years and split in half and was about the size of his forearm. He knew I was curious, so he let me heft the stave. It was heavy and solid. Then he explained that inside the stave was a bow, and it was his job to gradually take away the outer layers of wood until he found it.

From the perspective of a boy, the process of handcrafting a bow was tedious and time-consuming. First my grandfather scraped off the inner layer of wood beneath the bark, the pulp layer, then he shaped the rough outline of a bow with a hand axe. He removed wood from (what would be) the sides and the front, leaving the outer layer of grain, or the back of the bow, untouched. Then he began a more meticulous process with a knife. Because he worked on the bow only after his chores were done each day, the entire project, from start to finish, took at least a couple of weeks. That was an eternity for an impatient boy. When he did work on the bow, he worked slowly and carefully. But gradually, the bow emerged, as he said it would. It was about four feet long. In the middle, it was about two of his fingers wide and thick, gradually tapering to about the size of his little finger at each limb or wing tip. Then he built a fire using cottonwood and oak and waited until the hardwood burned down to glowing coals. Over the coals he held the bow, explaining that he was finishing the curing process and hardening the limbs.

In the final process of curing and hardening, he didn't talk about the bow. He talked about life. He talked about how each of us was like the bow he had made. Mothers and fathers and grandparents, he explained, and everyone who comes into our lives help make us into what we become. And there are times, he said, when life holds us over the fire. Those are the difficult times, but even the bad times can turn out to be good because they help make us strong.

I learned from my grandfather how to make bows and arrows. Each time I made a bow, I heard him talking about life. I always knew or sensed that my grandfather was a vast storehouse of knowledge, but there was a moment while making a bow that I realized how very wise he was. Almost in the same instant, I wondered if I would ever be wise.

Wisdom is a journey that begins the moment we are born. But as every wise person knows, there will never be a moment when we can say, "There, I am now as wise as I will ever be." Wisdom is a never-ending journey. There are times when still I wonder if I will become wise at all. How will I know when that transition occurs, if it does? I do know this for certain: Most of us accumulate the tools to be wise. The longer we live and the more experiences we have, the better our chances of becoming wise. But if wisdom is merely the accumulation of information that leads to knowledge, we can all be wise, because we all know something, and many of us are extremely knowledgeable in at least one area. Wisdom, I think, is more than information and knowledge. It is discernment, the ability to know when to apply that knowledge in a way that offers an answer or an insight.

When I was a boy, I fell through the top crust of a large snowbank because my grandfather allowed it to happen. He did tell me that a certain gully was filled with snow because of the large amount of snowfall that particular winter. But I had wanted to cross that gully to take a shortcut home. He could have grabbed me by the arm or the collar and taken me away from the danger, because he knew what would likely happen if I tried to cross the snow-filled gully. And what he knew would happen did indeed happen. I ignored his warning and insisted that I could cross the gully, and I fell through the top layer of crusted snow and down into the soft snow beneath. My grandfather pulled me out, of course, but I learned a lesson about snowbanks. More important, that experience was a lesson about wisdom. My grandfather knew that firsthand experience was the best teacher. He knew that I would never forget that incident and that it would one day give me an insight about wisdom. He was right. I will never forget swimming in that soft snow and being chilled to the bone, and I will certainly never forget the embarrassment. Years after the incident, I realized that falling down into that snow taught me how wise my grandfather was. He told me what would happen, and he allowed the situation to affirm his knowledge. Thereafter, I always took to heart anything he had to say.

Yet there is another profound lesson from that incident. My grandfather was giving back the gift that life had given to him. Wisdom is life's gift. Everything that has happened to us, and is happening, is life's way of giving us wisdom. Wisdom doesn't come from the amount of material gain we have accumulated; rather, it comes from the effort we expended to gain it. Wisdom doesn't come from the lowest depths we may descend to or the darkest moments we have and will know; it comes from the fall. And when we can look on ourselves and act without arrogance, no matter our material gain, we can be wise. If we can look past the disappointment and the failures and understand why and how they happened, we can be wise. Then we can, and will, give back life's gift.

There are still moments when I wonder if I will be as wise as my grandparents were. The answer is probably not. But close behind comes another thought: I can strive to be as wise as I can be. Now I understand, that was all they wanted me to learn.

There are many trails that crisscross the prairies and the valleys in the land of my boyhood. My grandfather and I walked many of them together. There is one trail that I must finish alone, however. The trail to wisdom. But both my grandparents showed me the way, and I will always do my best to follow.

About the Author

JOSEPH M. MARSHALL III is a teacher, historian, Lakota craftsman, and writer. He has authored several screenplays in addition to five books, including the highly acclaimed *The Lakota Way: Stories and Lessons for Living* (Viking Compass, 2002) and *The Journey of Crazy Horse: A Lakota History* (Viking, 2004). Joseph M. Marshall III is a member of the Rosebud Sioux Tribe and the recipient of the Wyoming Humanities Award. He has also appeared in the TNT miniseries *Into the West* and in the History Channel's syndicated program *The Real West*. To learn more about Joseph M. Marshall III and his work, please go to www.thunderdreamers.com.

SOUNDS TRUE was founded in 1985 with a clear vision: to disseminate spiritual wisdom. Located in Boulder, Colorado, Sounds True publishes teaching programs that are designed to educate, uplift, and inspire. With more than 600 titles available, we work with many of the leading spiritual teachers, thinkers, healers, and visionary artists of our time.

For a free catalog or for more information on audio programs by Joseph M. Marshall III, please contact Sounds True via the World Wide Web at www.soundstrue.com, call us toll-free at 800-333-9185, or write:

The Sounds True Catalog
PO Box 8010
Boulder CO 80306